BENN'S LONDON

EVERYONE'S LONDON · CULTURE · LEISURE
TRADING AND SHOPPING · PADS AND PALACES
RURAL LONDON · THE RIVER

for Thao

BENN'S LONDON

EVERYONE'S LONDON • CULTURE • LEISURE
TRADING AND SHOPPING • PADS AND PALACES
RURAL LONDON • THE RIVER

PHOTOGRAPHS BY OLIVER BENN

TEXT BY ANDREW EAMES

CONTENTS

End papers Part of the west facade of the Houses of Parliament.

Page 1 Left The dynamic art deco interior of the Odeon cinema, Muswell Hill.
Centre Faces from the Notting Hill Carnival.
Right The Dome, a gallery of classical busts, urns and antique fragments in the Sir John Soane Museum
(this photograph now © Soane Museum)

Pages 2-3 The River and city skyline at dusk, from the embankment near the National Theatre.

This page The art deco entrance hall in Unilever House, near Blackfriars Bridge.

First published in Great Britain in 1998, by Bouverie House, 66 Iffley Road, London W6 0PA

Photographs © Oliver Benn 1998
Text © Andrew Eames 1998

The photographer and writer have asserted their moral rights under the
Copyright, Design and Patents Act 1988 to be identified as authors of this work.

A catalogue record for this book is available from the British Library

ISBN 0 9532771 0 0

Designed by Maria Grasso, London

Repro by Colourpath, London   Printed and bound by Arnoldo Mondadori, Italy

PHOTOGRAPHER'S INTRODUCTION

Visually speaking, London is the richest city on earth. However, if you are looking for a memorable photographic essay, a search through the bookshops is a frustrating experience. The guide and travel books are scantily illustrated, if at all. The same applies to the historical volumes, and those focusing on particular aspects of the city. The touristic books do no more than recycle the familiar sights.

It was this gap in the market that made me feel that I had to do this book. There were so many more sights and symbols, so many new experiences out there which I was determined to record and to share. In some cases I knew they were there because I had seen or read about them, but mostly it was because I felt them as images in my mind, just as a composer hears melodies in his head.

Because photography is more a recording medium than an art form, it follows that a book of photographs stands or falls mainly by the choice of subjects.

This book represents my personal, sometimes unconventional selection, based on an ad hoc, seat-of-the-pants approach which developed into an ever more searching, year-long exploration, looking below the surface for the 'other' London, for the elusive spirit of this multi-layered, many-faceted city.

Sometimes the search led to wild goose chases. Sometimes the instinct which I have tried to develop, for being in the right place at the right time, failed me. On the successful occasions, however, I have attempted to produce entirely fresh impressions of a much wider range of London's lesser-known, unusual and exotic places and people than have hitherto been brought together in one book.

No essay on what is probably the world's most visited city would be complete without a sample of the well-known landmarks and tourist attractions, so I have included these in my first chapter.

Above and left These are some of the sights, sounds and living spaces I found in the 'other' London, which are more fully explored in my chapter on **Culture** (pages 30 - 53).

EVERYONE'S LONDON

London is a tale of two cities: the London that is familiar to Londoners, and the London that is shared between Londoners and the rest of the world.

This chapter holds the mirror up to shared London, the city of Big Ben and Tower Bridge, bowlers, bobbies and Beefeaters, black cabs and red double-deckers. All are symbols of a capital which ebbs and flows with 26 million tourists a year and two million commuters a day. This is the London that appears on the world's screens, in its guidebooks and in its magazines, the London of Royals, of Theatre, of Government, and of Work.

The hub of the shared city is Trafalgar Square, sending off spokes towards Royal London down the Mall, towards Official London down Whitehall, and towards the serious-minded City of London beyond the Strand. At its back is the fun-loving London of culture, shopping, eating and drinking.

Most of the year the layered square, which was named after a celebrated sea-battle, is a large and inhospitable traffic island, swirling with pigeons and

overlooked by Admiral Nelson on his column. But the square has taken its place in the nation's heart as the place to celebrate the victorious end to a war, to make a radical political point, or to welcome in a New Year.

It has a surprising tradition as a gathering place. Underneath its stones have been found the bones of cave lions, narrow-nosed rhinos and straight-tusked elephants, attracted here two million years ago by lush vegetation on the banks of the Thames. Today there's barely a window-box to be seen, and the river is invisible behind a deep wall of buildings.

The only erstwhile dinosaurs that still lurk among the canyon-like streets of Official London are the government departments, under the eye of Big Ben, the clocktower that may have got its name from a rather rotund clerk of works at the time of its construction.

The other symbol of government, Number Ten Downing Street, the residence of the prime minister, has been sealed off to the public for security reasons; a few years ago a salvo of mortars fired by the IRA landed in the back garden during a cabinet meeting. But you can still glimpse the occasional cabinet minister scurrying down Whitehall like the white rabbit in Alice in Wonderland, late for another very important meeting.

The Houses of Parliament themselves are not particularly old, but they can be impressive from across the river, or from the West when the evening sun glitters on diamond windows and picks out honeyed stone. It is said that Parliament was deliberately built with a river frontage so that it

Far left The hub of London, Trafalgar Square, with fountains by Edwin Lutyens, better known as the architect of New Delhi. The square itself was laid out in 1850 on what used to be a royal stables. In the background is the church of St Martin-in-the-Fields, over a hundred years older than the square.

Left A feisty horse leads Queen Boadicea's chariot along the embankment under the beady eye of the world's most famous clocktower, Big Ben.

could never be surrounded by the mob; certainly the river terrace is much liked by MPs, who can do their politicking in small groups over coffee, with little fear of being overheard.

Nothing is left of the densely-packed slums that once covered the Whitehall area. Today, these cavernous streets are empty by 8pm, when they revert to the realm of men and women of stone; Queen Boadicea, defeater of the Romans who originally colonised London, whips her chariot along the embankment beneath Big Ben without the benefit of reins, and Richard Coeur de Lion acknowledges the honking of passing traffic outside the House of Lords.

Across Parliament Square the largest and most eminent concentration of effigies is hidden within the walls of Westminster Abbey, where Official London comes together with Royal London at moments of birth, marriage and death. A large number of previous Royals rest peacefully here, along with prime ministers, scientists, playwrights and poets.

The focus of Royal London lies a short walk away through St James's Park. Buckingham Palace, or 'Buck House' in taxi-driver parlance, is the stony-faced residence of a monarch who has had plenty to think about in recent years, but whose expression has given famously little away. Although the Guard is ceremonially changed daily at 11.30am from May to August, and every other day otherwise, the Queen is here on average just seven months of the year. When she is in residence she is regularly visited by the Prime Minister, although she has little real influence on the affairs of government.

Part of the palace is opened to visitors during the Queen's annual Scottish holiday at Balmoral, and there's talk of increasing public access in general. Currently, the only time selected commoners are invited inside for tea and cake is for the huge Royal Garden Parties, although back in 1982 she was visited in her bedchamber by an intruder, and with remarkable sangfroid kept him talking while she summoned security.

Buckingham Palace lies about a half-mile west of Trafalgar Square. About the same distance to the east, the City begins. The journey between the two - up the Mall, along the Strand and into Fleet Street - is

a journey from royal London through aristocratic London to London's humble origins, although they are humble no longer.

What was once a maze of medieval trading-houses, so unruly that the Tower of London had to be built to keep them in check, has become an economic powerhouse with its own government - the

Corporation of London - and its own Mayor. The annual procession to mark the Lord Mayor's election makes a rare splash of frivolity in what is London's most serious Square Mile.

A more lively city begins north of Trafalgar Square. Dozens of theatres and department stores contribute to lurid, throbbing and heaving streets around

Leicester Square and Oxford Circus. This is the West End, focus of London's Culture, Leisure, and Shopping, all of which are the subjects of separate sections in this book.

These, then, are the focal points of shared London. But who gathers here?

As darkness falls, thousands upon thousands of migratory birds congregate in the trees above Leicester Square. Below them, equal numbers of people are coming together, but in a far greater variety.

The regular birds of shared London should have realised by now that few generalisations can be made about the human beings milling about below them. Probably the locals, in more dowdy plumage, will be in a greater concentration outside the Swiss Centre, underneath a clock that marks the key hours with a march-past with music; this is an acknowledged meeting place.

As for the rest of the animated, chattering throng who cluster like barnacles around a variety of street performers and evangelists, many of them will have migrated further to be here than any bird.

Even the Londoners waiting outside the Swiss Centre may not turn out to be what they seemed; the accent may prove to be Doncaster, it may be Devon, or it may be Hong Kong. Shared London has always had a magnetic pull for people with ability; it is where the nation's standards are set, and careers can be carved out with speed and fast reward.

Few Londoners really, truly, belong here. They scurry through the bright lights with barely a glance because they have some further goal in mind. Opportunity brought them to the city; they're young and in a hurry to get on. Then they get married - perhaps to that very same person whom they were hurrying to meet outside the Swiss Centre - and begin to appear less frequently downtown. Before long, there's talk of quality of life, of a house in the country. And then they are gone.

The notable exception to this rule is the real proud-to-be-a-Londoner cockney, supposedly born within hearing distance of Bow Bells, towards the East End.

Left The Angel of Charity, better known as Eros, presides over one of the most popular meeting-places in the world, Piccadilly Circus. Eros has had to be removed on several occasions, either for her own safety (as in the World Wars) or for a good clean.

Right Tower Bridge, in neo-Gothic style at the request of Queen Victoria, was opened in 1894. Its high level walkway became a haunt for prostitutes and villains and was closed in 1909. Eventually it re-opened as a tourist attraction, in 1982.

Right Life Guards wear bearskin hats (busbies) and make up the Queen's personal bodyguard, while bobbies - officers of the Metropolitan Police - are found on most city corners. Officers must, amongst other things, be able to swim 100 metres and have good eyesight. They are equipped with whistle, truncheon and handcuffs, and most also have a nice line in repartee.

Although comparatively few in number, cockneys make a disproportionate impact on the city by reason of their high-profile professions: costermongers loudly chiding each other from behind their stalls at street markets, or cab-drivers, giving a very idiosyncratic view of world events from behind the wheel of a black taxi.

The traditional sign of a cockney is his or her use of rhyming slang such as 'plates of meat' (feet), 'dog and bone' (phone) and 'trouble and strife' (wife). They have their own Royals, the Pearly Kings and Queens, so-called because their clothes are decorated with the poor man's mother-of-pearl: buttons. In October these costermongers' representatives return to Trafalgar Square for the annual harvest festival, but many will have travelled in for the day from new homes in places like Basildon and Milton Keynes, a long way from Bow Bells. Even the Pearlies move on.

Central London may be vibrant, but it is also ever-changing, as all fashionable places are. The great and the good were here, but like the Pearlies they left their mark and then moved away, with only a plaque to commemorate their passing. There's one in a narrow street in Soho, where Karl Marx wrote Das Kapital while staying in an upstairs flat; there's another just behind the railings beneath the Duke of York's column off the Mall, but this one commemorates Giro, a German alsatian.

This spirit of tolerance - celebrating a great Communist and a foreign ambassador's four-legged friend in equal measure - is one of the finest aspects of the city that belongs to the world.

But this is just the opening chapter of the tale of two cities. For the unfolding plot, the characters and the true setting of the story of London, you must dig deeper. Turn the page to the London that Londoners know.

Right Trafalgar Square, with the base of Nelson's Column and the church of St Martin-in-the-Fields. London's unique red double-decker buses provide a sight-seeing service as well as convenient transport.

Above and right
Often incongruously sited on London's streets and pavements, taxi-driver shelters are cosy places for a fry-up, a chat and a nice cup of tea. London's 20,000 black cab drivers are something of an elite; they spend up to two years acquiring "the knowledge", memorising London's streets, before being allowed to take the wheel.

Pearly Kings and Queens are the representatives of London's costermongers, traditional street traders. They gather annually for a harvest festival celebration in the church of the St Martin-in-the-Fields, on Trafalgar Square. Although officially cockneys, and therefore from the East End, many Pearlies have moved out to suburbs such as Thornton Heath (below right) or even further afield.

The Pearlies, so called because of the pearl-like buttons worn on their costumes, are ceremonial figures whose positions are inherited, not elected, and who often work for charity. The first Pearly, Henry Croft, was an orphan and a crossing-sweeper who made himself a suit of buttons in 1880, then sold it to raise money for a children's charity.

Above The Houses of Parliament are also known as the Palace of Westminster after a former royal residence on this site. The Palace used to be the main home of the monarch and parliament was housed in subsidiary chambers, but successive fires have re-modelled it over the centuries. Today's buildings date from 1840, and the Queen only visits on the occasion of the State Opening.

Right Previous royals maintaining a more permanent presence include King Richard I, Coeur de Lion, who rides through Old Palace Yard, just outside the House of Lords.

Far right Mounted troopers of the Blues and Royals at Whitehall are changed hourly.

Right The Horse Guards building is the office of the commander-in-chief of the British armed forces. Behind it is a large square, Horse Guards Parade, venue for regular military ceremonies. The annual royal parade, Trooping the Colour, ends here.

Below The Queen sets off in style for the State Opening of Parliament, one of several royal pageants in London's year.

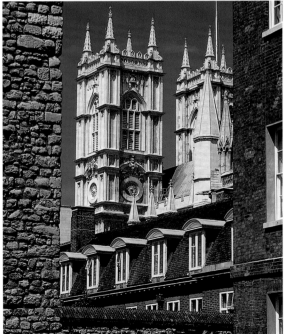

Left Westminster Abbey where the kings and queens of England have traditionally been christened, married, enthroned and buried. There is said to have been a church on this site, once known as Thorney Island, since 616. The present Abbey is mainly 13th century, although the towers are by Nicholas Hawksmoor, architect of many London churches, and were added in 1739.

Above The Queen Victoria Memorial in front of Buckingham Palace is a good vantage point for royal-watchers, topped by the gold figure of Victory, and with its creator Queen Victoria herself visible as the white seated figure on the left side of the central pillar.

Above The Queen's procession returns down the Mall from the annual State Opening of Parliament, held in late October or early November and also whenever a new Government is sworn in. In the right foreground is an allegorical group of statuary on the podium of the Queen Victoria Memorial, representing Peace and Prosperity.

Left Admiral Nelson looks down on passing traffic from 172ft above the square that was named in honour of his most famous victory, Trafalgar where he met his death. Trafalgar Square is surrounded by imposing official buildings, particularly Canada House and South Africa House, which was the focus of an anti-apartheid vigil which lasted several years. The square is the official centre of London, and a bronze plaque behind the statue of Charles II in the north-east corner marks the spot.

Left This imposing headquarters building by architect Terry Farrell on the riverside at Vauxhall was built for secretive residents: the British Intelligence Service, MI6. The design incorporates a Faraday Cage, which stops electro-magnetic information passing in or out of the building.

Left Queen Anne, in royal robes, overlooks Queen Anne's Gate, an elegant street off Birdcage Walk on the southern side of St James's Park. Queen Anne's Gate hosts the headquarters of the National Trust and the Museums and Galleries Commission.

Right Looking west from the top of St Paul's Cathedral, London remains remarkably low-rise, with the curved building on the riverside - Unilever's headquarters - one of the few that stands out. In the left background, the Thames turns south before passing Big Ben and the Houses of Parliament.

Below Once the home of the "hatch 'em, match 'em and dispatch 'em department" - register of births, marriages and deaths - Somerset House now houses the Courtauld Institute, with a fine collection of mainly French Impressionist and post-Impressionist paintings.

The Lord Mayor's Show, a procession through the City of London on the second Saturday in November, is a direct descendant of the medieval pageants which displayed the new Lord Mayor to the largely illiterate populace and also removed him from his City stronghold in order to swear allegiance to the Sovereign.
Above The procession stops at the steps of St Paul's Cathedral for the new incumbent to be blessed by the Dean.
Right Inflatable giants, Gog and Magog, the City's traditional guardians, on one of the floats.

Right The Worshipful Company of Mercers' float is based on its entry in the 1686 Lord Mayor's Show. Claire Eliot, goddaughter of the Company's Master, David Tate, portrays the Mercers' Maiden in her chariot - the Company's symbol and coat of arms.

Above The Tower of London complex from the north east. When Anne Boleyn (Henry VIII's second wife) was beheaded here in 1536, she insisted on being dispatched with a French long sword rather than the traditional axe. More recently, various spies caught during the two World Wars were executed within these walls.

Right The Tower still supports a garrison, with modern weapons.

Left One of the 40-odd Beefeaters ("Yeomen Warders") at the Tower of London. Traditionally drawn from the ranks of the army, today's Beefeaters (a name probably derived from the rations originally served to them) play a significant role as tourist guides.

Above Guarding one of the entrances to the City, also known as the Square Mile, are these Victorian wrought iron heraldic beasts mounted on the railings of Holborn Viaduct.

Left The Royal Naval College at Greenwich was built on the site of a former royal palace by Christopher Wren in 1664. It served originally as a seaman's hospital and now houses the National Maritime Museum. In the centre is the contemporaneous Queen's House, by Inigo Jones, whose recent restoration has recreated the original colours and materials.

Below Beyond it, on the opposite bank of the barely-visible river, are many examples of an altogether newer generation of architecture on what was once the Isle of Dogs; the Docklands development is symbolised by Canary Wharf, now London's tallest building.

CULTURE

"Little did I imagine that I would ever miss the bus to Hendon because of a Senegalese circumcision dance" - Richard Morrison writing in The Times, August 1997.

It would be almost impossible to sum up the cultural choice that London offers without resorting to cliché or hyperbole. Instead, I think the above quote - from a critic's review of a Promenade concert - gives some inkling of London's variety, and here are a few bald facts to help it along.

This is a city of 1,500 cultural events every week. A 'typical' year sees the curtain go up on a couple of hundred new productions in the West End, of which the majority are either classic or modern dramas. Amongst them Agatha Christie's *The Mousetrap* is now approaching its 50th year, while *Cats*, the longest-running musical, is merely in its late teens.

A large proportion of the more mainstream productions rely on a significant audience of overseas visitors. The latter tend to see less of the multitude of fringe venues - above pubs, in basements, and even travelling around the London underground - as well as of theatrical productions such as *Tales from a Mobile Bureau de Change*, described as 'an African music drama looking at the flamboyant excesses of London's Nigerian community'.

Right The clutter of antiquity in the Sir John Soane Museum has been left exactly as Sir John himself stipulated. The collection, some of which is his own work, is very ingeniously distributed through two town houses. (This photograph now © Soane Museum).

Below Much more recent and apparently less densely-packed is the entrance to the Clore Gallery extension to the Tate, the showplace of British modern art. Appearances, though, can be deceptive. The Clore Gallery was built to house the J M W Turner bequest, which consists of some 38,000 works.

Then there's a whacking 93 self-proclaimed comedy clubs (alternative comedy has been described as 'the new rock 'n roll'), not to mention all the nightclubs, art galleries and around 250 museums - the majority obscure and voluntarily run - all working hard to attract visitors.

Between them, these institutions house untold wealth in human creativity, both contemporary and historical. Only the tip of this huge iceberg can ever be displayed at any one time: take the example of one of the most celebrated and occasionally controversial galleries - The Tate - headquartered on Millbank but with branches at Bankside and elsewhere in the UK. The Tate's collection of British Modern Art is so large that only 3 percent can be shown in a year.

With such a quantity of cultural wealth in the city centre, it is all too easy to overlook anything that's a little further out, but two contrasting innovations are worth particular mention.

The Globe Theatre south of the river on Bankside looks ancient but was hand-built during the 1990s to simulate the Globe of 1599, in which William Shakespeare had shares. The audience is welcome to throw rotten tomatoes if it disapproves of the production.

The Globe is the fruition of one man's dream - actor Sam Wanamaker - who sadly didn't live to see it completed. Meanwhile the new home for the British Library (next to the old St Pancras railway station) is the fruition of years of government prevarication. Originally commissioned back in 1962, the first stage didn't finally open until 1997, with a final bill to the taxpayer of £500 million, hugely beyond even the wildest estimates. Still, the library does hold the largest collection of printed material in western Europe, and it is good to have given it a home of its own - albeit one that Prince Charles described as looking like an academy for the secret police.

Prince Charles would undoubtedly be far more fulsome in his praise of two more traditional temples of culture. The Sir John Soane Museum is, like the Globe, the result of one man's passion. Sir John was a bricklayer's son who rose to be architect of the Bank of England, with magpie tendencies for any form of creativity of his time. He died in 1837, leaving a peculiarly personal collection at 13 Lincoln's Inn Fields, which includes a Monk's Cloister in the garden, which he built from architectural fragments that he himself rescued from the old Houses of Parliament.

Also the result of one man's eclectic magpie tendencies - but with a rather broader horizon - is the Horniman Museum in Forest Hill, south London. Frederick Horniman, Quaker tea merchant with missionary connections, believed firmly in the merits of eating rice pudding every day, even when travelling the world. Wherever he went he couldn't resist the souvenirs, from musical instruments to nomads' boots. And this is the basis of his collection - exotic souvenirs from before the souvenir trade really began. Eventually, his house became so overcrowded, both with what he collected and the people he invited in to see it, that his wife reputedly set him an ultimatum: "either the collection goes or we do". So in 1901 the art nouveau style Horniman Museum was completed; interestingly, it is one of the few in London that still offers free admission.

The whole business of free entry to museum collections has aroused much debate in recent years. Many feel passionately about making all London's accumulated cultural wealth as accessible as possible.

Although the battle against admission charges has largely been lost - with the exception of the British Museum - there have been some notable successes in the general principle of widening the audience for art. One of the most celebrated is the annual series of 70 Promenade Concerts, which take place between July and September. The Proms were created way

Above and right The original Shakespeare's Globe of 1599 was built south of the river so as to be outside the city's jurisdiction. This recently completed replica is very faithful to the original, with an open roof, standing room for the audience, and an invitation from its artistic director to "eat, drink, laugh and cry, or just listen, look and imagine with a freedom unlike that of any other theatre."

Above Scene from Shakespeare's *A Midsummer Night's Dream* in the open-air theatre in Regent's Park. The open-air theatre season runs from May till September, and dates back to 1932. Although the majority of performances are classical drama - mostly Shakespeare - there are also open-air musicals.

Left For something more challenging, London's many fringe theatres, often attached to pubs as here, at the *Canal Café Theatre* in *The Bridge House* pub in Delamere Terrace W2, offer a variety of strikingly unconventional performances.

back in 1895 to bring music to a more diverse public by selling cheaper tickets for standing room only - as was and is done in both the Globe Theatres, old and new.

The cheap ticket policy combined with challenging programming (including the Senegalese circumcision dance) has created a whole new culture of Promenaders who are not in the conventional mould of music lovers. They often dress eccentrically, and spend the intervals shouting obscure messages from the floor to the gallery of the Albert Hall. The last performance of the series inevitably turns into a riotous singalong with silly hats and flying toilet rolls, to the disapproval of the more sober-minded.

A portable version of the Proms has been appearing in London's parks in recent years with the assistance of Government and Lottery money. Colourscape is an inflatable labyrinth with 96 chambers of intense colour and musicians playing at its centre. As in the Proms, the audience is free to wander around.

Without Government funding such imaginative ideas would find it hard to get a public outing. There are plenty of very active independent artists in London, particularly in studios around the East End, but their work is rarely seen by the general public. People like Andrew Logan making huge sculptures in his converted garage the Glasshouse, and artist Ricardo Cinalli who works in the shadow of Hawksmoor's church in Spitalfields.

Only a limited selection of London artists will be shown in one of the Bond Street or Cork Street art galleries; one or two might appear in one or other of London's public spaces, and a few more will be in the catalogue of Sotheby's the auctioneers - but only after they are dead.

But without such people, of course, the culture of London would have no animation. The fountain of culture is people, and the sort of mixture of people who have adopted London as their home make that fountain particularly vigorous.

Back in 1955, a mere 500,000 international passengers passed through Heathrow airport. By the mid-1990s that figure had increased to 48 million. Few of today's arrivals will realise that the airport was originally built by construction workers shipped in from the Punjab. They are more likely to notice that a large proportion of the staff on the Underground are West Indian, that the street corner newsagents are often called Patel, and that the sandwich shop proprietors speak to each other in either Italian or Greek. It's not surprising that the city's favourite dish, the staple of 3,000 restaurants and staff canteens, is not roast beef - it's curry.

London is where the parochial English meet the movers and shakers of the rest of the world. In no fewer than 12 inner London boroughs the majority of school pupils are non-white. This city has 33 resident ethnic communities of more than 10,000 people who were born outside the United Kingdom, and still more of smaller size. These days the door is officially closed to new immigrants, but relatives are still arriving in their tens of thousands every year.

Naturally enough all these races sponsor all sorts of religious beliefs. London has scores of synagogues, temples and mosques, although not all are as unmistakable as the Wat Buddhapadipa temple in Wimbledon, which looks as if it has stepped straight out of the pages of an illustrated guide to Thailand. The very diversity that these ethnic communities bring to the streets is a major part of the city's attraction.

Even Christianity comes in several forms: the more traditional, with some churches such as St James's Piccadilly thriving, and others struggling; and the happy-clappy variety, packed to the gunwales with an emotional congregation whose singing regularly raises the roof.

Below Sumptuous interior of the Hackney Empire, designed by Frank Matcham in 1901.

Matcham created over 60 theatres in his time, and was known for his flamboyant style.

Above and left
The Royal Albert Hall echoes the design of Roman amphitheatres. Built in 1867-71, it can hold up to 8,000 people and hosts everything from boxing matches to prayer meetings. Its most celebrated series are the Promenade Concerts (**above**), which date back to 1895 but regularly break the conventions of classical music both in choice of programme and in the audience they attract.

Far left Contemporary, and unconventional in terms of setting, are the musical performances in Colourscape, a 96-chamber multi-coloured inflatable labyrinth which tours London's parks in the summer. The audience, themselves wearing cloaks of primary colours, are led "on a journey where music and visual art meet".

Above and top right
A group of street artists from Australia called *Strange Fruit* perform their bizarre pole-bending aerial ballet on the terraces outside the Royal Festival Hall (RFH), the largest building in the extensive South Bank arts centre near Waterloo. There is usually some sort of free live performance either outside or inside the RFH at lunchtimes during the weekends.

Right Art in the open: picnickers attend a summer concert on the lawns leading down from Kenwood House on Hampstead Heath, in typically unreliable weather. Concerts usually come to a stirring climax after dark, sometimes with a musical firework display.

Left The Odeon Cinema, Muswell Hill: the building itself is art. The Odeon's art deco interior dates from the 1930s, the era of the explosion in the number of picture palaces throughout the country. The original doors and light fittings have survived, and the present carpet was specially designed to harmonise with them.

Left Commercial culture: the auction room at Sotheby's of New Bond Street, where paintings and other works of art regularly set record prices. Despite the exclusivity of big money, anyone is free to attend an auction.

Left Detail of the interior of the Gala Club which also dates back to the 1930s. A former cinema turned bingo hall in Woolwich, the decor is in the Venetian Gothic style.

Below The new British Library on Marylebone Road was designed by architect Colin St John Wilson, with the mock-Gothic turrets of the old St Pancras station rearing up behind. Around 12 million volumes are stored in four levels of underground basements beneath the reading rooms of the new library, and hundreds of new books are researched here every year. The spacious piazza in the courtyard includes a small amphitheatre for open-air performances.

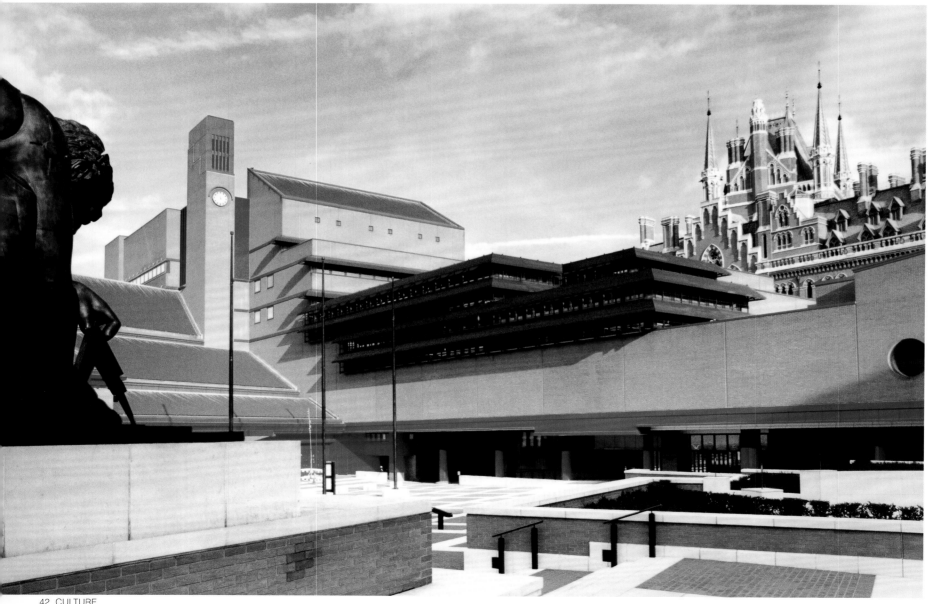

Left and above
It will be some time before readers accustomed to the echoing old quarters in the British Museum adjust to these silent, clean-limbed interiors and the library's computerised book ordering system.

The Glasshouse in Bermondsey, home and studio for sculptor Andrew Logan and architect Michael Davis. **Right** Part of the studio. The brilliant, saturated colours of the walls were achieved by using the same paint that King Ludwig of Bavaria used for his Palaces.

Above On the bedroom wall hangs a collection of portraits and photographs of friends.

Left The exterior of the Glasshouse, converted by Davis from a former garage and workshop. The name derives from the glass roof, on the left, built over the studio.

Above Andrew Logan and an assistant working in the massive, top-lit studio, a hot house environment of mirrors, resin and glass. His work ranges from huge, flamboyant sculptures to costume jewellery. His surreal art, in which Mexican and Spanish influences are prevalent, has caused him to be described as the "Wizard of Odd."

Left The stark, cuboid sunken studio of artist Ricardo Cinalli in Spitalfields. It was excavated under what used to be the back garden of his house, formerly a derelict dairy, and provides a sky-lit workspace dominated by the spire of Hawksmoor's church. The drawing on the end wall is entitled *Defeat* (1989).

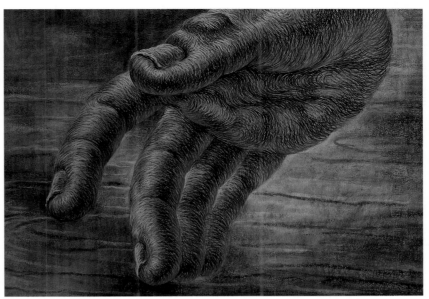

Above A detail from one of Cinalli's large-scale drawings, executed in pastels on super-imposed layers of tissue paper.

Cinalli's second floor bedroom/bathroom (**above**), a room which he sees as an "installation". He has fixed chunks of plaster to the walls to create a substantial trompe l'oeil scheme based on classical sculpture.

IS LIFE A BOON?
IF SO IT MUST BEFAL
THAT DEATH WHENE'ER HE CALL
MUST CALL TOO SOON.
W.S.GILBERT

Above A partly-robed muse leans against the plinth of a statue of Victorian composer Sir Arthur Sullivan in Victoria Embankment Gardens, a strip of green between the river and the Strand.

Above Staircase entrance to the striking art nouveau Horniman Museum, opened in 1901 in the south London district of Dulwich. The mosaic on the facade represents the course of human life. The Horniman itself started life as tea merchant John Horniman's personal collection of rare and curious objects from all over the world. It has kept that wide brief, while specialising in ethnography, natural history, and musical instruments.

Centre An allegorical group of neo-classical statues from 1797 stands in the 16-acre gardens, which also contain a glass-roofed conservatory and a grass-roofed ecologically designed study centre for the environment.

Right In the new-look Kensington Temple - or KT to its congregation - it is standing room only, and the focus is on creative ministry, satellite links, the love of Jesus, and instant healing.

Right The faithful at evening prayers in the Great Mosque in Brick Lane, in the East End. The striking, classical-style interior has been previously a Huguenot church (from 1743), a Wesleyan chapel, and an ultra-orthodox Jewish synagogue. Brick Lane was once a centre of Jewish London, but is now a focus for the Bengali Muslim community.

Left A service in St James's Church, Piccadilly, which dates from 1684. Designed by Sir Christopher Wren, St James's represents conventional Church of England services.

Left In the Buddhist Wat Buddhapadipa in Calonne Road, Wimbledon, one of the missionary monks receives small gifts from pregnant Thai ladies, following which he blesses them and their unborn children.

Right The exterior of the Wat Buddhapadipa, a gift from the King of Thailand which was assembled according to traditional Thai specifications by a British builder.

Left and below The Buddhas of Battersea: lying and standing Buddha details from the Peace Pagoda, which was erected by the riverside in Battersea Park in 1985 by Japanese monks.

LEISURE

The city that works hard, plays hard. West End theatres, cinemas, restaurants, pubs and nightclubs are heaving with people throughout the year.

Going out to eat or drink are staple forms of urban entertainment, and in London there are around 5,500 restaurants and a similar number of pubs to choose from. The restaurant choice is not always easy: a nation not noted for its cuisine created a vacuum that has been filled by the cuisines of the rest of the world. It is often said, for example, that Chinese and Indian cooking in London are better quality than they are at home. In recent years the biggest boom has been in Thai, Singaporean, Indonesian and Malaysian restaurants.

Good eating is common to most cities in the world, but there is one particularly distinctive form of recreation that is very London, and also takes place in the West End - albeit behind closed doors. The tradition of gentlemen's clubs, particularly along the length of Pall Mall and in Piccadilly, is a long one. Most were founded in the 18th century, when men and women of breeding led separate social lives. The club started as somewhere for the gentlemen to eat roast meats in the company of like-minded fellow members. Meanwhile the ladies developed their social life around the home. But then restaurants began to develop, tastes for society life and for cuisine became more sophisticated, and the club lunch got rather left behind.

In their prime there were about 900 traditional clubs; today there are barely a couple of dozen left. One of the most celebrated is the Athenaeum, a glorious quasi-Grecian construction by Decimus Burton on the junction of Pall Mall with Waterloo Place. The Athenaeum was named after Athena, goddess of wisdom, and intended as a meeting place for men who enjoy the life of the mind. Dickens, Conrad, Kipling and Thackeray were all members, and the club's roll of honour includes 40 Nobel prize winners. The concept of "blackballing" - to reject by a vote - was invented here thanks to a ballot system for new members which used black and white balls. The word has entered the English language and the voting system is still in use.

The spirit of the Athenaeum - a gathering of like-minded, high-achieving professionals - may be old,

but it is visible today in the emergence of a new kind of London club. The Groucho, Soho House, Momo, and Circus also emphasise shared and sophisticated interests. Age profiles of these clubs are generally far younger, and their dining sometimes more adventurous.

As far as the average Londoner is concerned, though, the local pub is the closest he or she will get to a club life. Most London pubs date from the late 19th century, and were built to impress by wealthy brewers, offering far more grandeur and elegance than was found in most homes. Like the clubs, they started as largely male-only territory, and their licensing regulations - opening only at lunchtime and in the evening - kept the families away.

But the pub has changed. The relaxing of opening restrictions, combined with competition from wine bars and an emergent cafe culture, has created a more flexible pub environment. Many have diversified into food, and this is usually where British cuisine pokes its head out from behind the kitchen door.

Right The imposing stairway of the Athenaeum on Pall Mall, founded in 1823 as a club for leading "scientific and literary men and artists" and designed by Decimus Burton.

Below The club was named after the Greek goddess of wisdom, Athena, whose golden image stands outside.

Left The Athenaeum library where William Thackeray wrote several of his books. Some of the Club's more traditional rules must still be observed; for example, it is forbidden to discuss business or take any paper out of your pocket in the dining room.

Below The frieze around the Club's facade is a copy of the Elgin Marbles, originally from the Parthenon and now in the British Museum.

In the busy pubs of central, shared London you're unlikely to be buttonholed by someone keen to discuss whether Rome was really built in a day. Start to move out of the centre, though, and you begin to get a more typical pub life, with regular customers and distinctive entertainment. Pubs double as theatres, quiz houses, sports clubs and music venues. Choose carefully and you could sip your pint of hand-pumped London Pride - London's most well-known local beer - while enjoying the banjo-led mayhem of a Russian gypsy trio from Khabarovsk. Or you could attend one of the gatherings of the Cogers, a debating society that dates back to 1750, and holds regular meetings every Saturday in the Betsy Trotwood pub on Faringdon Road to discuss the week's events.

Clubs and societies are thick on the ground in any British region, and London is no exception. Almost every form of sport can be practised locally, from Octopush (a form of underwater hockey) and Korfball (a Dutch variation on basketball) to Aikido, a form of harmonious martial arts "for mental,

spiritual and physical attributes" using a wooden staff and wooden sword, taught in a hut in Hillingdon.

Then there are London's festivals, of which the most celebrated of recent years is also Europe's largest street party: the Notting Hill Carnival. Every August bank holiday up to two million revellers fill the streets to watch a parade, which originated in Trinidad but now encompasses the whole of black London.

Of the purely spectator events, football easily leads the pack. London teams such as Chelsea, Arsenal, Crystal Palace and Tottenham have huge followings, and well-known international stars in their ranks. Surprisingly, greyhound racing is not far behind in terms of popular following, and most of the big London stadiums have a dog racing night or two during the week. In the post-war years going to the dogs was a major pastime; these days the crowds have shrunk to hundreds rather than thousands, but most will loyally attend every meeting and carefully

Right Meanwhile, the nearest most ordinary mortals get to a gentleman's club is their local pub. The pub pictured - *The Flask* in Hampstead - is a tied house, which means that all of its beer comes from one brewery, in this case Young's of London.

Right *The Albert* on Victoria Street is known for traditional British roast lunches.

Above Exteriors are made as attractive as possible, and their signs can be real works of art. This detail is from the *The Cross Keys,* Covent Garden.

Above *The Bunch of Grapes* has a well-known restaurant, and is located in Shepherd Market, the select area of village Mayfair that once had a dubious reputation.

Above Typical London pub interiors are made up of dark wood, mirrors and high ceilings as in *The Man in the Moon* in King's Road, Chelsea.

follow every dog's form in the hope of a successful bet. And as for the on-course bookmakers, they have a language all of their own.

In winter, high society gathers like something out of the old movies in hotels like the Waldorf and the Savoy for Sunday afternoon tea, sometimes with dancing. Londoners with less cash in their pockets but an equally strong desire to relive the good old days take their partners in Stratford Town Hall. For the more modern community, spas, gyms and swimming pools come into their own. The 1930s picture palaces have long since either become multi-screen cinemas, bingo halls or thriving music venues.

In summer London's extensive canals become a major place of recreation.

A jazz session in *The Bull's Head*, attractively situated on the river in Barnes and one of Europe's best known modern jazz pubs. The first session was in 1959 and many leading artists have appeared here since then.

You don't have to be a jazz lover to drink in the bar at
The Bull's Head, which originally opened in 1672. The present
building is early Victorian. With their regular clientele, pubs like
this act as a focus for the local community.

Right Greyhound racing at Walthamstow Stadium. The dogs chase an electric hare at speeds of up to 40mph, and individual performances are carefully monitored by the regulars, with a view to next week's betting. On-course bookies, their stalls down by the rail, have a language all of their own.

Right A Cogers debating society meeting in *The Betsy Trotwood* pub on Faringdon Road. The society dates back to 1750, and the regular Saturday night debates start with an opening speaker, who selects his own subject from the week's events. Members occasionally travel to away fixtures - debates with other societies from further afield.

Left Old Time ballroom dancing in Stratford Town Hall, in the East End. The Hall is a fine example of Victorian craftsmanship, with eight chandeliers and an impressive plaster ceiling.

Faces from the Notting Hill Carnival, where just wearing the costume, let alone walking in it, can be quite a feat of endurance. Started by the expatriate Trinidadian community as a reminder of home, where carnival marked the end of slavery, today's street party takes place on the first weekend in August. Carnival was originally a preparation for Lent (and is still widely celebrated as such), and pancake tossing was the original carnival activity, symbolising the using up of rich ingredients which had to be foregone during Lent. Abstinence is not, however, the salient quality of the Notting Hill event.

Right Once a fruit and vegetable market where monks from Westminster Abbey would sell their produce, Covent Garden was saved from demolition in the 1970s by a vigorous group of local residents. Since then the 170-year-old market hall has become one of London's biggest attractions, with a rich variety of shops, cafés and entertainment.

Right For grandeur in a fresher location, the *Villa dei Cesari* is located on the riverbank in Pimlico, between Chelsea and Vauxhall bridges. The ambience is elegant, the arches Moorish, and the food is Italian.

Above The *Il Sarastro* restaurant in Drury Lane, which describes its richly ornate decor as "neo-Ottoman" to complement its Turkish-oriented but eclectic menu. The main dining area seen here is overlooked by balconies like opera boxes, with rich velvet curtains.

Above Contemporary restaurants such as *Stephen Bull's Bistro* in St John Street, EC1, have moved on from the small-portioned, ornate nouvelle cuisine that was all the rage a few years ago. Stephen Bull (once the chef, now the managing director) emphasises good quality raw materials in the restaurant's modern cuisine, featuring dishes such as Moroccan fish stew and salt cod pie.

Above Casual eating at *Ed's Diner*, an American chain of themed café restaurants which is spreading through London. Eating out in London is not just a matter of what you eat, but where you eat and what you wear while you're eating.

Left Blissfully steamy: London is not known as a health resort, which is why the art deco *Porchester Spa* plunge pool in Queensway comes as something of a surprise. *The Porchester* comes complete with gym, swimming pool and Turkish baths, and is unusual in that it is run by the local borough. You pay at a wooden kiosk at the entrance.

Above and right A more luxurious and exclusive centre of health; the *Dorchester Spa* in the eponymous hotel. (Open to members and hotel guests only). This spa is also in art deco style, but was opened in 1991, and emphasises treatments to de-stress the body and re-balance the system.

Above and left
One of the prettiest sections is in Maida Vale, and is known as Little Venice, where a whole community of barge enthusiasts live on board their boats. One-quarter of the UK's 400 residential houseboats are in London.

Left The 8-mile Regent's Canal (shown at Camden), runs between Paddington and Limehouse Basin in Docklands, and was only completed in 1820. The first suggestion to have it filled in to make a road came just 25 years later, in 1845. Fortunately, that pressure was resisted, and today it is possible to walk 40 miles along canal towpaths in London.

TRADING & SHOPPING

"I am still unable to decide whether The City is a person, or a place, or a thing... You read in the morning paper that the City is 'deeply depressed...' at noon it is 'buoyant' and by four o'clock it is 'wildly excited'." Stephen Leacock (1869-1944) in *My Discovery of England*.

Mr Leacock's is an understandable confusion. The City (note the capital "C") is where the place called London actually began. Part of the original 2nd century wall around Roman Londinium still remains. This area is quite distinct from the region of shared London where most tourists congregate, usually referred to as the West End, which grew up around Westminster.

Subtitled London's Square Mile, The City is the home of international banks - at the last count there were 561 of them - the insurance business and the law, as well as shipping, multi-national holding companies and more. It has its own police force (officers don't have to be as tall as in the Metropolitan Police), its own local government, its own ancient trade associations, and it has even managed to keep its Lord Mayor while the other boroughs had theirs swept away in the Margaret Thatcher years.

The City is hugely powerful both in the UK and abroad, but it doesn't wear its heart on its sleeve. For the average visitor it is little more than a confusing labyrinth of tall stone monoliths jammed forehead to forehead on a medieval street pattern. Seeing no real joy in pediments, porticoes and premium policies, most visitors barely tarry on the journey from the West End to the Tower of London - a fortified dungeon originally built by the king to keep the unruly mob of the City in check.

But there's a very distinctive atmosphere to these stone-clad streets. During the day they are thick with scurrying messengers and red buses; in the evening they are blurred with pinstripes and black taxis; by night they are practically deserted. Despite the Barbican centre - an early attempt at a condominium now largely used as a pied-a-terre by folk whose main residence is elsewhere - fewer than 5,000 people live in the City.

Left One of the sumptuous food halls in Harrods, which started life as a grocery store in 1934. Today many Knightsbridge residents still regard Harrods as their local corner shop.

Above The heart of the City, where the Bank of England (left) faces the Corinthian portico of the Royal Exchange (right). The equestrian statue is of the Duke of Wellington.

It was not always so. Once upon a time 200,000 people lived in galleried half-timbered houses hanging over narrow lanes, with all the trade taking place in markets and shops below. The Fire of London of 1666 did a great clearance job. Remembered today by the Monument and the statue of a golden boy in Cock Lane, the fire initially prompted the then Lord Mayor to remark, scornfully "a woman could piss it out" - words he was later to regret. By the time it was spent, it had reduced 13,000 houses and 89 churches to ashes. But from the ashes came a significant phoenix: an architect by the name of Christopher Wren.

Much of Wren's work was later completely destroyed in the Blitz of World War II, although miraculously his St Paul's Cathedral survived while all around it was flattened. The Cathedral did receive a direct hit, but the bomb didn't go off. Instead, it was carefully extracted, taken beyond the city limits and detonated, leaving a crater more than 100 ft wide.

Thanks to the Blitz, the City today is dominated by buildings of the post-war years, with a few nuggets of history - including some churches by Wren - propped up between the monoliths. But the street names are still redolent of the very beginning: Threadneedle Street and Sea Coal Lane, Bread Street and Poultry. These are the commodities that used to be brought up the Thames in sailing barges, to be unloaded on the wharves of the Pool of London.

The Livery Companies set up in 1514 to regulate these early trades also still exist; but the original 12 - Mercers, Grocers, Drapers, Fishmongers, Goldsmiths, Skinners, Merchant Taylors, Haberdashers, Salters, Ironmongers, Vintners and Clothworkers - have increased to a hundred, including new disciplines such as information technology. Few have much direct interest in those businesses their names suggest, but they remain powerful groups of businessmen, with ancient meeting halls and traditions, whose main external activity is the sponsoring of charitable interests.

There is only one hangover of the City's earliest trading years still active, but Smithfield Meat Market's days in its galleried hall beyond the Old Bailey (the Central Criminal Court) are numbered. Once upon a time this was practically countryside, and cattle were herded down the byways that led to its back door. Now the lorries arrive overnight from the furthest reaches of Europe, and there's talk of relocating Smithfield away from the centre.

Although there are still exclusive Edwardian and Victorian shopping arcades in the West End - notably the Royal, Burlington and Piccadilly arcades - the only other structure in the City that dates back to the era of buying and selling on the street is the shell of Leadenhall market. The Victorian framework has been nicely preserved, but inside it functions as a place of leisure.

This Boy is in Memmory Put up for the late FIRE of LONDON Occasion'd by the Sin of Gluttony 1666

Trade has moved on. Today the commodities that used to fill the stalls in the likes of Leadenhall have been replaced by their paper or electronic representatives, way away from street level.

Although the modern City institutions still deal in many of the same basic materials, they do so in massive quantities by computer, often as Futures before the commodities have even been baked, quarried, or grown, and certainly without them coming anywhere near the United Kingdom.

Nevertheless there are some hangovers from the original way of doing business. The gesticulating, colourfully-dressed dealers on the floor in the Futures Exchange (LIFFE) and the Metal Exchange are sometimes from a cockney background, the likes of whom would have once been buying and selling energetically on the pavement.

But there's old money behind many institutions, no matter what they look like. In an uneasy combination of old and new, the City's huge insurance business - the biggest in the world - operates from Richard Rogers' Lloyd's Building on Lime Street. This striking tangle of tubes conceals a honeycomb of insurance brokers and underwriters. Behind them all, taking the real risks, are the Names - private individuals who are prepared to put their wealth at the disposal of Lloyds' market experts, with long-term profit in mind. Recent years, though, have been hard on the Names. A few have maintained that they were badly served by the market experts, and have refused to pay.

The 1980s boom broke the boundaries of the Square Mile, and the City spilled out to colonise huge areas of disused port land to the east. Spectacular new developments shot up along defunct former wharves, and the revitalisation of Docklands, with all the interesting new architecture it produced, was the inner-city development story of the decade.

But Docklands investors, like the Lloyd's Names, suffered badly in the recession that followed. Even Canary Wharf, Docklands' signature building, was barely a third filled. Today, a decade on, it has benefited from the transplant of the media business from Fleet Street and the picture is looking a lot healthier.

Industry per se has long since gone from London. Shopping is the biggest contributor to the economy, followed by tourism. Both are united in the West End department stores, each with its own niche market, and each a community in itself. A store like Liberty's on Regent Street, which specialises in fabrics, has some 500 members of staff. Peter Jones, on Sloane Square, is run by an unusual survivor in modern business: a family-based co-operative.

The most celebrated of the traditional department stores is Harrods of Knightsbridge, its facade lit by 11,500 lightbulbs and decorated with the royal crests of its more upmarket customers. Some 35,000 people pass through these doors on a typical day to be served by 4,000 staff; over 12 million distinctive

OPFERQUE · PER · ORBEM · DIÇO

Each of the City Livery Companies has its own Hall, many of which have managed to survive both World Wars and Great Fires, and carry their Companies' coats of arms above the entrances. **Above** The Apothecaries Hall. **Below** Saddlers Hall, with an appropriate motto for horsemen.

Far left The statue of a small boy in Cock Lane commemorates the Great Fire of 1666.

Left One of the casualties of that conflagration was the original Royal Exchange, founded by Sir Thomas Gresham in 1564. His bust adorns the ornate entrance gates.

HOLD · FAST ✦ ✦ ✦ SIT · SURE

Right The glass-roofed, arcaded Leadenhall Market houses traditional meat and game dealers, croissant and coffee shops, and a pub frequented by City men and women after work.

Right The trading floor at the London International Financial Futures Exchange (LIFFE), where financial risks are still bought and sold in the traditional way.

green and gold carrier bags are taken home every year. Besides the new Egyptian staircase, its most remarkable section is the food hall, both for the artistic presentation and the variety on display. Harrods' motto is "all things, for all people, everywhere" and it does stock a huge range, as well as being able to get anything else. As for the "for all people", that's a more debatable claim. This has always been the store for high society, and teenagers of good breeding are often taken on for holiday jobs,particularly during sale periods. If you want to be served by a marquess in the making, then Harrods is the place to go.

Beyond the central area of London the shopping returns to where it started in the early years of the City - to the street. To the East is Brick Lane market (Sundays only), perhaps the cheapest of the lot, and with plenty of cockney characters. To the south is Brixton Arcade (daily), at the heart of the West Indian quarter, and selling everything from worrybeads to breadfruit.

To the north is Camden Lock (Saturday and Sunday), weekend mecca for anything and anyone remotely trendy or arty. And to the west is Portobello Road (Friday and Saturday), where the cream of all the other markets might eventually end up, highly polished, highly priced, and elegantly displayed.

Overleaf A City panorama, from the Nat West Tower on the left through to the illuminated Lloyds building on the right. Despite the innovative modern architecture, the City still follows the same street pattern as it did in medieval times. Just 5,000 people live in the Square Mile, but a further 350,000 arrive for work here every day.

Left Just off Leadenhall Market is the London Metal Exchange, another rare survivor of a traditional trading floor but with soberly dressed dealers using ritual gestures.

Right Richard Rogers's Lloyds Building at the corner of Lime Street and Leadenhall Street, opened in 1986 but still strikingly futuristic. Sometimes seen as a work of engineering rather than architecture, it is most impressive when lit up at night.

Above The Lloyd's insurance market was started by a gathering of merchants in Edward Lloyd's coffee house in 1688. Seen here is the weekly management meeting at Stace Barr Ltd., members' agents. Each of the directors looks after the interests of a number of underwriting Names.

Left A traditional sailing barge at Heron Quay in the Docklands, with Canary Wharf Tower in the background.

Left The multi-storey, top-lit atrium at Liberty on Regent Street, with a variety of oriental rugs on display. Founded in the 19th century by Arthur Liberty, arts patron and expert in foreign silks, it has diversified into a wide range of other materials.

Above The mock-Tudor facade facing Great Marlborough Street was completed in 1925 using the timbers of two old battleships.

Right The art deco barber's shop in the basement of Austin Reed, Regent Street. Department stores are often complete villages in themselves, offering every possible service under one roof.

Left and above Their precursors are the covered shopping walkways such as the highly-decorated Royal Arcade, an idea that was borrowed from continental Europe at the beginning of the 19th century. The arcade became "Royal" with the permission of Queen Victoria, who used to shop at Bretell's at number 12.

Right The clockwork figures representing Mr Fortnum and Mr Mason greet each other on the hour on the facade of the high-class store in Piccadilly which bears their name. Assistants in the grocery department still wear frock coats.

Top left The exclusive glass-roofed Burlington Arcade, on Piccadilly, pictured at Christmas time, is policed by uniformed beadles, usually retired servicemen. Rules include no running, singing or unseemly behaviour.

Above Also seasonally decorated, the Piccadilly Arcade is just across the road, and specialises in china, rare books and clothing.

Left and right
Sales by design: central London stores have to be properly dressed, as in these eye-catching window displays at Simpson Piccadilly. Window-dressers are mostly young art school graduates keen to make a name for themselves. They often work through the night to get their creations ready for the morning rush-hour.

Above The impressive display of fruit in Harrods food halls.

Right Their fish display, below the mermaid figures, incorporates
a new design of fresh fish each day.

Above The Columbia Road Market in Shoreditch on Sunday mornings is one of the best in London for flowers, plants, bulbs and seeds. The site was previously occupied by the huge Victorian Columbia Market building, erected to provide the local community with a place to buy cheap and nourishing food.

Petticoat Lane, actually in Middlesex Street near Liverpool Street station, is perhaps London's most famous street market. **Left** The traditional garments from which its name derives. **Above** Some of the stalls display a variety of household ornaments as well as the clothing and leather in which the market specialises.

Left and above
Retailing may be moving onto the Internet, but Petticoat Lane seems to have been able to ignore the threat of the digital superhighway. This is still the heart of the rag trade, and it provides an interesting cross-section of all the different ethnic communities living, working and shopping in the East End.

LOCK ONE
LONDON
BATIK ART
GALLERY

ORIGINAL
BATIK
PAINTING
BY HAND

OPEN →

MORE SHOPS
UPSTAIRS

FIRE EXIT

Carnivorous
Plants

LOCK ONE
LONDON

Left The ornate Victorian market hall at Camden Lock. This building and the three adjacent cobbled yards now house numerous small shops, studios and stalls, where young designers can market fresh, experimental styles of clothing and crafts.

Above and right On the south side of the river, the Brixton Arcade may seem exotic to most casual visitors, but its contents are essential shopping for Brixton's West Indian community.

PADS & PALACES

When London first became the uncontested capital of England, the choice of how and where to live was a clear-cut question of birthright. Either you were rich and lived in a massive town house within hailing distance of the royal palaces and government around Westminster, or you were poor and lived in a slum in what is now the City. But urban fires were no respecter of wealth, and it wasn't until stone became more extensively used in the Tudor era that buildings began to survive.

As London began to grow faster, however, its centre became increasingly focused on the activities of merchants, which the true gentry found irksome. So they moved outwards to build mansions in country surroundings.

Left The Brann marketing consultancy occupies a Georgian house in Soho Square. Inside, though, the decor (as in the reception area, shown) belongs to an altogether different era, and far better suits the image of a contemporary creative business.

Right No such liberties have been taken with Hampton Court Palace, where the interior is as carefully preserved as the exterior. Here the Georgian south wing, by Sir Christopher Wren, overlooks the formal Privy Garden.

The trend-setter was Cardinal Wolsey, who started work in 1514 on a rambling Tudor palace at Thames Ditton, with the intention of rivalling the royals. This was a pretty provocative thing to do, especially as Wolsey failed to get Henry VIII the divorce he wanted; Wolsey hastily gave Hampton Court to the king in an attempt to revive his own career, but it was too late.

Henry appreciated Hampton's riverside setting as a perfect weekend retreat, and the house was added to by him and a succession of other monarchs. Soon, aristocratic families who wanted to be within reach of both town and country courtly life began to build at regular intervals along the banks of the Thames; Osterley Park, York House, Syon House, Marble Hill, Chiswick House, Ham House, Orleans House and more - all are within reasonable distance of each other. These houses' semi-rural locations saved them from the fires, bombs and redevelopment schemes of central London.

One of the best preserved is the creation of Horace Walpole, MP and man of letters. While retaining his town house in Berkeley Square, Walpole bought an old house in Twickenham in 1747. It took him another 44 years to transform what the locals called Chopp'd Straw Hall into his splendid neo-Gothic

Strawberry Hill. Within are some of the finest interiors in London, modelled on outstanding medieval cathedrals and castles.

Even in Walpole's own day the house became so celebrated that he began to get fed up with casual visitors asking him to give them a tour, complaining that they tried to "see with their fingers" - in other words, they touched things.

Meanwhile, the city itself had started to be developed for gracious living. When it was built in the last years of the 17th century, the new St Paul's Cathedral was still within sight of fields and orchards. But it wasn't long before they too began to disappear under the grand squares of Mayfair and St James's, designed by architects like Robert Adam. One of Adam's creations was Apsley House, right on Hyde Park Corner. When it was completed (1778), Hyde Park Corner was on the outer limits of the City and Apsley's address was Number 1, London.

London's population at the end of that century was just 900,000 and did not require a huge urban area. But the story was to change dramatically in the course of the next one hundred years, during which the number of Londoners increased more than sevenfold to 6.5 million.

Right A quiet cul de sac in Bywater Street, off King's Road, Chelsea, which started life as a fishing village. As London developed, "quaint" Chelsea became a centre for artists and writers.

The twin engines behind this hugely accelerated growth were the industrial revolution, and trade with a rapidly growing empire. Much of the latter had started to come up the Thames to London, and some of it was being processed at the city's heart. Sugar cane from the West Indies, for example, was refined within a mile of the riverbank, and then took ship again, sometimes even back to the West Indies. These industries needed workers, clerks and middle-managers, and quickly. And all of them needed housing.

The new professionals and entrepreneurs did not, yet, have the wherewithal to build themselves country piles, nor could they afford to distance themselves from the world of work. So they compromised on London's new squares and started to colonise former villages just beyond the existing urban boundaries.

Chelsea, Notting Hill, Hampstead, Islington, Dulwich and Richmond all became fashionable

places to settle. These villages allowed access to work and urban delights, but only as and when desired - a take-it-or-leave-it attitude towards central, shared London which persists in village London even today. Most of them have long since been surrounded by urban sprawl, but the village pond could still be there, and there may still be Sunday cricket on the green.

At the same time the workers were finding accommodation in whole new suburbs of terraced housing marching across the countryside. This great sprawl was only possible thanks to the coming of effective public transport. The Underground Railway ("the Tube") was started in 1863, when London had a radius of 4 miles. Today the Tube travels up to 27 miles from central London, carrying 2.5million passengers every working day.

But London is no longer growing. The population reached a peak of 8.5 million in 1939, and has now

declined to 6.9 million, thanks to the decline in inner-city industry. There have been distinctive benefits: the last pea-souper smog was in the 1950s, slums have gone and former factory sites and warehouses have been attractively converted to fashionable accommodation in a process nicknamed gentrification.

Shared London doesn't make a good living room, though. These days most of central London's oldest formerly residential buildings have been redesignated with some sort of business or official function, as embassies, institutions or clubs. One former town dwelling that does open its doors to the public (Sundays only) is Spencer House, just off St James's Street, which was built by Earl Spencer - an ancestor of Diana, Princess of Wales - back in 1756, and has recently been gloriously restored.

The current process of warehouse conversion is typical of London's patchwork development. This city has little of the homogeneity of Paris or

Amsterdam. Only one person has really ever impressed some sort of uniformity on it: the architect John Nash. His scheme for a utopian garden city had the Prince Regent's support (it is said that the architect's wife and the Regent were "friendly"), but he soon ran into entrenched conservatism elsewhere, and only the Regent's Park part of the scheme was completed. Some of his work, particularly Regent's Street, was later altered.

These days there's a frustration amongst modern architects with London's essentially conservative attitude to town planning. Were it not for the bombing during the Blitz in World War II, today's architects would have found it hard to make an impact in central London. Many of the modern buildings in the City and surrounding areas were built on sites destroyed in the war. Architects like Norman Foster and Richard Rogers have had to do much of their major work overseas. And when they do come up with a plan for a new building in central London, they may well have to contend with the

present Prince of Wales - Charles - who is notably outspoken against what he sees as the shortcomings of modern design. Although he has no real political power, his opinion has become a major influence in what does and does not get built.

So many of the older central London buildings remain untouchable in structure, and survive as urban scenery that is poorly suited to the contemporary purposes of their occupants. Some of the latter have taken to reflecting something of their identity by creative ideas within, as in the case of marketing consultancy Brann who occupy a listed Georgian house in Soho Square. The restrained period exterior belies the explosion of colours within.

In domestic buildings, and away from the city centre, architects have been allowed a freer reign, as in the cutting edge examples of contemporary housing in Holland Park and Deptford shown on pages 120-121.

Where to live in London is still an abiding concern, even 500 years after Cardinal Wolsey turned the face of London society by building Hampton Court. This is the city where house prices pay more attention to the subjective elements of social cachet and desirability rather than to more tangible amenities such as the number of rooms, the square metres of floorspace and the distance in miles to the city centre. The result is that a house in Richmond can cost twice or three times as much as a house in Shepherd's Bush, despite the fact that the latter is some 4 miles closer to Piccadilly Circus.

Anomalies like these ensure that pads or palaces, owned or rented, remain a talking point of which Londoners never tire.

In the 18th century another politician had his own private palace tailor-made: Horace Walpole, MP, bought a modest house in Twickenham and spent 44 years converting it into neo-Gothic mansion Strawberry Hill. The exterior is a virtual encyclopedia of architectural styles. Each change in parapets, window shapes, roof outlines, chimneys, turrets, etc is a reference to a specific European building that Walpole particularly admired. The overall result is what Walpole called "Sharrawaggi" - deliberately unsymmetrical. It was very much out of line with the neo-classical style in vogue at the time.

Left An architectural magpie, Walpole had the staircase hall at Strawberry Hill modelled on the library stairs at Rouen Cathedral, and the wall tracery based on a design found on the tomb of King Arthur in Worcester Cathedral. The original colours were much darker, to achieve a sort of romantic melancholy.

Top The library is very much as Walpole intended it, and is also lent a sepulchral air by the pierced Gothic arches above the fireplace and bookcases. The chimney-piece is in imitation of a tomb in Westminster Abbey, and amongst the extensive library are 48 volumes of Walpole's letters.

Above The chimney-piece in the Holbein Chamber is also a copy of a cathedral tomb, that of Archbishop Wareham at Canterbury. The room was originally a bedchamber, and got its name from twenty paintings by Holbein that once hung there. The ceiling, of *papier maché*, was copied from the Queen's

bedchamber at Windsor. The delicate tracery of the screen partitioning (left of picture) is based on a screen in Rouen Cathedral, which was burnt down later in the eighteenth century. Walpole was a great collector, but he also had an eye for the frivolous, complaining once that he had been outbid for Oliver Cromwell's night cap.

Above The Great Hall at Syon House (on the river between Brentford and Isleworth), as re-modelled in the mid 18th century by Robert Adam. The large bronze in the foreground, *The Dying Gaul*, is a copy of an antique statue, as are the other statues around the walls. In earlier times, two of Henry VIII's wives, Catherine Howard and Lady Jane Grey, were confined here before their executions. Later, the body of the Monarch himself lay in state here en route to Windsor, but was partly devoured by a pack of hounds during the night.

Left Frolicking Italianate maidens in the gardens of York House, Twickenham are thought to be re-enacting the birth of Venus.

Left The house itself was built in the late 17th century, and its most celebrated early occupant was the Lord Chancellor the Earl of Clarendon, who used to stay here while his boss King Charles II was in residence at Hampton Court. Today only the gardens are open to the public.

Above Intended for entertaining rather than for living in, Chiswick House was built in 1729 for the third Earl of Burlington. In the style of a Palladian country villa, it housed much of the Earl's art collection. In the early 20th century it became a mental institution, before being restored to its former glory and opened to the public, with some of the original art back in situ.

Above The gardens were also based on an Italianate design, and along with this Ionic temple include closely hedged walkways each leading to different landscapes. Woodland, formal gardens, an orangery, lakes and a cricket pitch are all tucked into a comparatively small area.

Left The house and gardens become the focus for several arts events in summer, particularly the open air theatre, with performances of Shakespeare in August.

Left Spencer House, overlooking Green Park and dating from 1766, was the London residence of the Spencers of Althorp, Northamptonshire. As at Chiswick House, the neo-classical exterior is more than matched by the sumptuous detailing of its interior (**below**). One of the first floor reception rooms, the Painted Room (**far left**) was much admired and imitated at the time (the furniture is on loan from the Victoria & Albert Museum).

111

Above The Palm Room at Spencer House, originally called Lord Spencer's Room, is one of the suite of ground floor apartments which were designed by John Vardy, a disciple of William Kent, and illustrate the transition from Palladianism to Neoclassicism. It has a dramatic screen of corinthian columns forming palm trees, whose gilded leaves reach across the arches.

Above The carving on the chimney pieces is also of outstanding quality, as in this detail of a phoenix.

Left One of the ornate gilded doorhandles in Spencer House, here in the Great Room on the first floor.

Above One of London's oldest surviving timber-framed buildings, Staple Inn, on High Holborn, was built in 1545 as a hostel for wool merchants. The upper storeys and strip windows are typically Elizabethan. Before the Great Fire, London's streets were lined with many such buildings.

Far right Unmarked by the march of time, Pickering Place is a secluded square reached through an alley off St James's Street. The houses date from the early 18th century.

Right Crusader effigies from the 12th and 13th centuries rest in Temple Church, by the Inns of Court off Fleet Street. The original round church dates from 1185 and is one of only five such left in Britain.

Above Regency fanlight from an 18th-century house in Bedford Square (**left**) at the heart of Bloomsbury. Originally laid out by the Earl of Southampton, Bloomsbury became a stronghold of creativity thanks to the likes of Charles Dickens, John Constable, George Bernard Shaw and Dante Gabriel Rossetti, who all lived here.

The Bloomsbury Group was formed at the beginning of the 20th century by Virginia Woolf and artist contemporaries who wanted to challenge the conventions of the day. Today these quiet squares in the shadow of the British Museum and the University of London are the traditional home of the book publishing industry.

Left Grand Georgian houses overlooking Kew Green. Many were built for members of the King's Court during the reign of George III, and were used while the monarch was in residence at Richmond Palace.

Above Corporate chic: The elaborate entrance hall-way in the Express Newspapers building (**right**) at the south end of Blackfriars Bridge.

Right The huge Unilever building, on the site of the former Bridewell Palace on the embankment by Blackfriars Bridge, was built as a corporate headquarters and still functions as such. Completed in 1932, it has some striking Art Deco interiors, as here in the entrance hall.

Far left Modern
movements: Form
follows function in the
home of Page Starr, a
dramatic conversion of
a traditional mews
building in Holland
Park.

Above and left
Minimalism is the order
of the day at this small
private house and
garden, a converted
former grain store in
Deptford, south east
London.

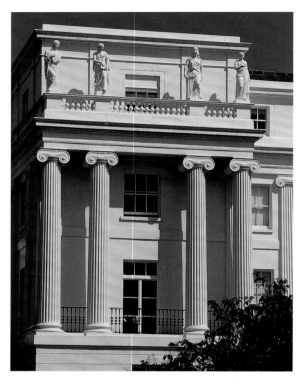

Corinthian columns and statuary at the centre of Cumberland Terrace (**far right**) and balancing one end (**right**). The terrace was built along the east side of Regent's Park in 1827 by John Nash, who was more interested in its visual impact across the park than in the detailing of its interior, which he left to others. Although the impression it gives is of one huge palace, there are in fact several residences and several separate entrances.

Below The semi-circular Park Crescent was originally intended to form a complete circle. Some of Nash's work - notably Regent Street - was later undone by the Victorians, who called his work monotonous and ridiculed his extensive use of stucco.

RURAL LONDON

Urban tourist boards around the world place heavy emphasis on their native green space, and London is no exception. Indeed, some poor soul in the financial square mile has been instructed to count the trees ("almost one thousand") to show how rural that is, too.

Whether London is greener than any other capital city would be hard to prove. Statistically, its parkland covers 30 per cent of the Greater London area. And if that seems a lot, it isn't even the whole story. Urban green space comes in all shapes and sizes, not all of which can be described as "parks". For a start there is the never-ending jigsaw of private back gardens, many of which are a true labour of love. Then there are the 95 golf courses inside the M25, the ring road around London, as well as dozens of football pitches and several village greens where cricket is still played in summer.

Above The sunken Pond Garden at Hampton Court was created by Henry VIII in the 1530s, and is one of several different green spaces from different periods at the palace. Amongst other highlights are a vine that dates from 1796 and the famous Maze from 1714.

Right The Chelsea Physic Garden on Royal Hospital Road and Swan Walk has long had a beneficial impact on the health of the city. It was founded by the Society of Apothecaries in 1673, for the study of the therapeutic properties of plants.

All these patches of greenery are the lungs of the city, filtering out carbon monoxide and exchanging it for oxygen. Indeed, one of London's green spaces - the walled Chelsea Physic Garden - was specifically created back in 1673 for the growth of herbs to improve the nation's health.

But the therapeutic value of parkland is more than that. The parks are great levellers, and on the whole their interest lies less in horticulture and more in the life you find within them. You can share a bench with an oriental potentate, a politician or even a member of the Royal family, with roller-skating rock stars whizzing past you down the path. Even burial grounds, like Brompton cemetery, which ramble over scores of acres, are used for recreation - or for browsing through the curious inscriptions on headstones.

The best known London green spaces are the Royal ones: in the centre that means Hyde Park, Regent's Park, Kensington Gardens, and St James's Park, all of which were once the property of the sovereign, but which have now been turned over to public use under the watchful eye of the Parks Police.

St James's Park is most like a royal front garden, sitting between Buckingham Palace and the government offices of Whitehall. It was created out of boggy land by Henry VIII, and stocked with deer for decorative purposes. In temperate weather you can see a variety of civil servants and business men and women sunning themselves during their lunch break. There are usually a surprising variety of waterbirds, including pelicans, in the lee of the government buildings, and a minister's dog, Buster, recently landed his master, former MP Roy Hattersley, in court by making a meal of a royal duck.

Hyde Park is less formal than St James's, although it merges almost seamlessly into the more carefully-crafted Kensington Gardens, whose palace was strewn with flowers during mourning for Diana, Princess of Wales.

Hyde Park, like St James's, was also created by Henry VIII. It hosts, inter alia, demonstrations, rock concerts, baseball tournaments and fairs. Every winter a hardy collection of swimmers plunge into

Right A rose garden on Christchurch Street, a rustic corner of Chelsea.

its lake - the Serpentine - on Christmas Day. Every summer the park welcomes flocks of migrating Arab families, their womenfolk moving through the trees like hooded black birds.

To the north, Regent's Park contains the London Zoo - on the brink of closure a few years ago until it was rescued by a Saudi prince - the Open Air Theatre and the Central London Mosque. Its pastoral-looking lake was the scene of a tragedy during the cold winter of 1867, when the ice gave way under the weight of skaters and 40 people drowned. Since then, the depth has been reduced to 4½ feet.

Overall, Regent's Park is a carefully landscaped piece of scenery which nicely contrasts with the encircling grand terraces created by architect John Nash. Nash was only really concerned with views and facades; he left the internal structures to others.

Regent's Park was the eye of his utopian scheme for a massive and elegant garden city, with a palace for the Regent in the park itself. Like much of the rest of the scheme, the palace was never built.

The scenic juxtaposition of brick and stone with carefully landscaped greenery is found in formal squares throughout central London; best known are probably Soho Square, Berkeley Square, Belgrave Square and Golden Square, but there are dozens more. Most of their central gardens are fenced off, for private keyholder access only, but they are so open to public scrutiny that they are very rarely used.

People prefer to go somewhere where they can lose themselves in a mixed crowd - as in Hyde Park - or where the green space is so extensive that it has the feel of real countryside. There are four celebrated places where you can do the latter, in ascending order of size: Kew Gardens, Hampstead Heath, Wimbledon Common, and Richmond Park.

The Royal Botanic Garden at Kew, at 300 acres, is the most carefully landscaped of the four, but with some 33,000 varieties of plants there are plenty of corners in which to get lost. Kew also has two impressive glasshouses, a Chinese pagoda, a Japanese Gate, and a Dutch-style palace.

Hampstead Heath, twice the size of Kew, rolls over hilly ground north of the centre, and on a clear day you can look across to the hills of Crystal Palace in the south. The Heath is known for its open air bathing pools - one for men and one for women - and for a series of summer concerts on the lawns outside Kenwood House, which sometimes end in a dramatic display of fireworks and music. On its eastern side is Highgate Hill and Highgate cemetery,

where celebrity graves stand draped in tangles of wildflowers and romantically gloomy shrubbery.

South of the river is Wimbledon Common, 1,100 acres of rough land with surprisingly dense woodland and a windmill at its heart.

Biggest of all the London spaces is Richmond Park, twice the size of Wimbledon Common at 2,500 acres, and with several distinct areas of woodland, a golf course, a couple of lakes and 250 red and 350 fallow deer spread over a clump of hills. This is the largest city park in Europe, and perhaps the only one where a deer cull has to be carried out by stalkers with guns. In Richmond's woodland, surrounded by the bellowing of rutting stags, it is easy to forget you're in London at all - were it not for the roar of Pratt & Whitneys overhead, as jumbo jets full of new arrivals descend towards Heathrow.

Above Church Walk cottages bring rural England to the heart of Richmond.

Left Flowers in the front garden complement the blaze of colour of a doorway in Harrow, in north west London.

Right At dusk artificial light picks out the trees in St James's Park, and couples sometimes linger there in summer.

Right Charles II stands in Soho Square, an oasis of quiet in what is otherwise a rather rumbustious area of London. The square was laid out in the 17th century, although the mock Tudor gardeners' shed at its centre is from the 19th century, and conceals steps leading down to a large underground cavern.

Left The vista across St James's Park towards the government offices of Whitehall. St James's started as a royal deer park in the 1540s, but it owes its present shape to architect John Nash, working at the behest of George IV. At the far end of the lake is Duck Island, a bird sanctuary, with resident pelicans.

Right Berkeley Square, where nightingales supposedly sing, is well shaded by huge plane trees. The square was laid out in 1747 by William Kent, and Queen Elizabeth II was born in a house on the east side in 1926.

Left Middle Temple Hall, shown here in its garden setting, is unblemished by time. It was built in 1576. Its fine hammerbeam roof and beautifully carved Elizabethan oak screen are regularly enjoyed by the barristers who work here. The Hall is occasionally open to the public.

Left Roses grow in what used to be the nave of Christchurch Greyfriars, in the City of London. Christchurch, which was designed by Christopher Wren and destroyed by bombing in 1940, is actually the second church on this spot; the first was destroyed in the Great Fire of 1666.

Above The Little Cloister Garden in the precincts of Westminster Abbey.

An eclectic variety of architecture can be found in Kew Gardens'
300 acre site. The great glasshouses (the Temperate House and
the Palm House) defy the onset of winter, but outside the seasons
follow their natural course, as here (**above**) at the
Temple of Aeolus, the Greek god of winds and dwellings, built on
a small hill in the 1760's.

Left The lake at Kew Gardens in autumn. Since the Gardens were started in 1759, 33,000 different types of plants from all over the world have been collected here, and in some cases re-distributed, as with bread fruit trees to the West Indies.

Left In summer, cricketers colonise the Kew village green near the main entrance to Kew Gardens.

Although it only opened in 1839, Highgate Cemetery swiftly became very popular with the noble and the notable. There is a romantic gloom in this tangle of funereal urns and shrubbery, and it has attracted poets, novelists and actors, including Christina Rossetti, George Eliot and Sir Ralph Richardson.

The overgrowth (**left**) is deliberate; some 250 different species of wildflowers (**far left**) have been introduced, as well as countless trees and shrubs, sometimes giving a splash of colour (**below**). The cemetery comes in two halves; the western side (tours at specific times only) is maintained by the Friends of Highgate Cemetery while the eastern side is open daily and funerals still take place there. The most famous tomb of all is that of Karl Marx, who lived out his last years in London, and is in the eastern cemetery. It bears the inscription "workers of all lands unite".

Above Curiosity corner: A little-known feature of Hyde Park, the
Pet Cemetery, is tucked away behind Victoria Gate Lodge
adjoining Bayswater Road. It began in 1881, when the
gatekeeper, a Mr Winbridge, agreed to bury Cherry, a Maltese
terrier belonging to a family who visited the Park regularly, when
she died of old age. Many of the dogs buried here met their end
by being trampled under the feet of the horses in the Park. The
cemetery was officially closed in 1903.

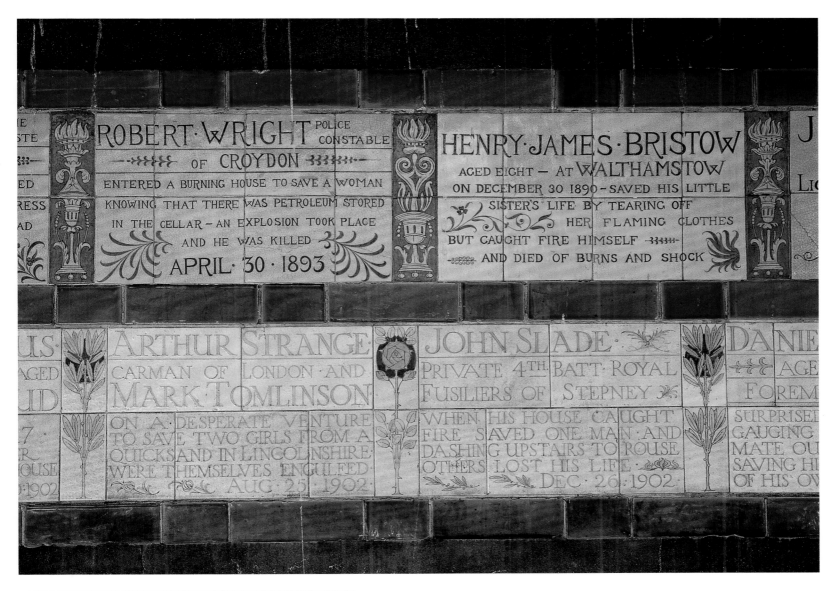

ROBERT · WRIGHT POLICE CONSTABLE
~·~·~ OF CROYDON ~·~·~
ENTERED A BURNING HOUSE TO SAVE A WOMAN
KNOWING THAT THERE WAS PETROLEUM STORED
IN THE CELLAR — AN EXPLOSION TOOK PLACE
AND HE WAS KILLED
APRIL · 30 · 1893

HENRY · JAMES · BRISTOW
AGED EIGHT — AT WALTHAMSTOW
ON DECEMBER 30 1890 – SAVED HIS LITTLE
SISTER'S LIFE BY TEARING OFF
HER FLAMING CLOTHES
BUT CAUGHT FIRE HIMSELF
AND DIED OF BURNS AND SHOCK

ARTHUR STRANGE
CARMAN OF LONDON · AND
MARK TOMLINSON
ON A DESPERATE VENTURE
TO SAVE TWO GIRLS FROM A
QUICKSAND IN LINCOLNSHIRE
WERE THEMSELVES ENGULFED
AUG · 25 · 1902

JOHN SLADE
PRIVATE 4TH BATT · ROYAL
FUSILIERS OF STEPNEY
WHEN HIS HOUSE CAUGHT
FIRE SAVED ONE MAN · AND
DASHING UPSTAIRS TO ROUSE
OTHERS LOST HIS LIFE ·
DEC · 26 · 1902

Above Equally curious is Postman's Park, a small former burial ground off Newgate Street, so-called because postmen from the nearby General Post Office used to come here to eat their sandwiches. The wall bears a series of plaques commemorating ordinary men and women who died in heroic attempts to save others.

Left The flowers of Spring. Each year Kew Gardens celebrates the re-birth of Spring with a profusion of flowers: first crocuses, then daffodils (shown left), then the many other flowers of late spring and summer.

Right Autumn comes to Wimbledon Common. Evidence of Neolithic man's presence has been uncovered here, and the land has been in common useage ever since records began, although the pasturing of animals has had to be limited because of poor soil. At the heart of the common is a 19th century windmill built by a local carpenter, and now a museum.

Left Hampstead Heath's Kenwood House was created in 1764 by Robert Adam for the Earl of Mansfield. It contains the Iveagh Bequest of paintings, and looks down towards the lake where midsummer concerts take place.

Left The river bank at Chiswick, that supports a variety of swans, ducks and other aquatic birds.

The Thames from
Richmond Hill, looking
towards Isleworth, in a
very pastoral scene that
is nevertheless in the
heart of suburban
London. Upstream from
here the river is no
longer affected by the
tides.

THE RIVER

Every great city in the world has water at its heart, and London is no exception. The river Thames may not be as wide as the Amazon or as long as the Danube, but it is a ribbon of constancy through a city of change; hobbyists with metal detectors are often seen on shingle banks laid bare by very low tides, where they recover surprising souvenirs dating back to Roman times.

At 209 miles from source to mouth the Thames is the third longest river in the country. From Teddington Lock downriver it is locally known as the Tideway, for obvious reasons: at certain stages of the moon, tidal changes can make it seem both in danger of flooding and practically empty on the very same day.

It is by no means an easy waterway to navigate. The tide can be remarkably strong in either direction, and this partly explains why it is so little used as a leisure resource. Sailing is only permitted for two hours on either side of high water, and even then you have to be sure of enough wind to have the edge over the tidal flow, or you will be in danger of being swept into the estuary.

The river's banks are a great attraction, particularly those stretches with well-loved pubs at Putney, Hammersmith, Strand on the Green (Chiswick) and Richmond. On a fine day these sections of the towpath are brimming with people.

On the Tideway itself, rowing is the biggest pastime, with two races with international appeal every year: The Head of the River Race for eight-oared boats usually attracts more than 400 entries, many from Europe, and practically no spectators. The Oxford and Cambridge Boat Race, on the other hand, has only two entries - but a worldwide audience of millions. The attraction of the Boat Race is hard to fathom, because the outcome is often decided in the first minutes of the two-horse 20-minute race, but it nevertheless has a well-established place in the sporting calendar.

At their peak, these two university crews could take on the best in the world. But perhaps more important is the sheer tradition of an event which started back in 1829. In the early days the attention may have been on the university gentlemen, but they were by no means the fastest on the river: the race was refereed from a boat rowed by Thames Watermen, who had to keep up with the racing crews despite carrying the extra burden of the umpire.

Being a Thames Waterman was a way of life even up to the middle of the 20th century. In the years after World War Two there were still 30,000 employees of the port of London, and 7,000 lightermen manoeuvring barges and cargo boats up and down river. The Pool of London, just upriver from Tower Bridge where the museum ship HMS Belfast now lies, was so thick with boats that you could practically walk from one side of the river to the other.

In its first year of operation, 1894, Tower Bridge was opened 6,160 times. Back then there were 55 miles of active wharves and quays in London's docklands.

Left A bit more youthful than Richmond Bridge but equally striking is Chelsea Bridge, an early suspension design from 1858. Golden galleons with coats of arms stand on top of the bridge pillars at the entrance.

Right Richmond Bridge was completed in 1777 and is the oldest river crossing still in use, but the classical-looking development on the river bank is in fact by contemporary architect Quinlan Terry and dates from 1988.

Above Enjoying the sun on Strand on the Green, Chiswick, where the towpath is lined with pubs and Dutch-style gabled houses.

But as the sun set on the British Empire and ships grew larger and more unmanoeuvrable, the docks up the winding river began to wane. By the 1960s they were all but derelict. Today, Tower Bridge lifts a mere 600 times a year, mostly for leisure craft.

Of the few true watermen who remain, most are in the tourist boat business based at Westminster Pier. From here the most popular journey is downriver, past the Traitor's Gate through which prisoners were delivered to an uncertain fate in the Tower of London, through Tower Bridge and along the gleaming towers of now-revitalised Docklands to Greenwich, where much of the nation's nautical history is recorded in the Royal Naval College, the

mothballed sailing ship *Cutty Sark* and the National Maritime Museum.

All these attractions hearken back to the time when the river was a major thoroughfare - instead of just a flightpath for helicopters. There have been attempts to make it an active transport link again, most recently in the 1980s with the launch of a fast ferry service to link the new Docklands area and City Airport with the West End. Sadly, it didn't attract enough business to survive. In fact the only remaining ferry is up at Twickenham, where Stan Rust carries foot passengers across the river in his boat *Peace of Mind*.

Below
More pubs line the riverbank at Hammersmith. The suspension bridge was opened in 1887 and has been strengthened twice since then, but has not managed to keep up with the demands of modern traffic. It is currently closed for further improvements.

Below right The oarsman's view, looking back towards the bank from underneath Hammersmith Bridge, is also a peaceful one.

Other, more permanent, structures have long since taken over the job of transporting people and vehicles from one side to the other. There are 31 bridges and 11 tunnels across the Tideway, although not all are in active use.

The very first London Bridge was built by the Romans sometime after AD43; it was massively rebuilt in stone a thousand years later, with houses and shops incorporated into the structure, and it remained the only permanent river crossing until Westminster Bridge was built in 1750. Since then there have been two more London Bridges on the same site, and one of them has been rebuilt in Lake Havasu City, Arizona.

While the recent bridges have a more slender footprint in the water, that early medieval bridge was so massive that it was almost a dam. The slow flow had two effects which are not often experienced these days. In winter, the river would freeze over, and ice fairs were frequently held on its surface. In summer, it failed to carry away the sewage of a swelling population. Even Parliament had to be abandoned during the Great Stench of 1858, caused by a heady mix of sewage and industrial pollution.

Today the river has been narrowed by the introduction of embankments to accommodate roads above and underground railways below, and the effect has been to greatly accelerate the water flow.

Above right For safety reasons, sailing is only permitted on the Thames two hours either side of high tide - and the tide can be very high here: all these Chiswick houses have well-used flood defences.

Above Dusk on the 75-berth marina in the Chelsea Harbour development, which was built on a former coal depot in the lee of Chelsea Power Station. Chelsea Harbour, with over 300 apartments including one owned by Michael Caine, was a pioneer in a recent spate of riverside initiatives, turning land that had been used for wharves and warehouses into residential and office accommodation, as the river has reverted from industrial to leisure use.

For evidence of how the width has been reduced you only have to look to the Strand, which once ran along the water's edge. Now it is at least 100 yards away.

Upstream, the changes have been less dramatic. The city's oldest extant bridge spans the river just above Teddington Lock; although it was built in 1774-7, Richmond Bridge still carries a heavy traffic load.

Thanks to a decrease in industry, to fewer boats, and to more thoughtful sewage arrangements, today's river is far cleaner than it ever was. Instead of a rank, busy thoroughfare, it is an oasis of peace, now remarkably thriving with natural history. Salmon are back, and anglers complain bitterly about the increasing numbers of fish-hunting birds. People live happily in boat-based communities alongside Chelsea, Hammersmith, Chiswick and Richmond, and in recent years a seal has been spotted swimming up through Central London.

Great care is paid to the welfare of water life. In dry summers when the river's flow becomes unhealthily turgid, a large, mysterious flat-bottomed boat moves slowly upriver. From the outside it looks as if it might be scanning the riverbed for Roman treasure, but in fact it is blowing bubbles at the fish.

Right A few brave souls still live on boats opposite Chelsea Harbour, although these days there's little evidence remaining of Chelsea's origins as a fishing village.

Left Downriver from Chelsea Harbour is Albert Bridge, seen here from Battersea Park. It is a typically ornate Victorian suspension bridge which comes dramatically to life when lit at dusk.

London has been subject to flooding from surge tides since before 1236, and as recently as 1953 one of the worst recorded floods claimed 300 victims. Eventually the Thames Flood Barrier (**above**), a remarkable combination of modern architecture and engineering, was built between 1972 and 1984 to address the problem. Its ten moveable steel gates weigh from 400 to 3,700 tonnes each.

Above The shoulders of Terry Farrell's massive Embankment
Place, seen here from the terrace of the Royal Festival Hall, rise
over the river by the Hungerford rail and foot-bridge, between
Westminster and Waterloo. The office building conceals
Charing Cross station at its heart.

Above Looking across the river towards the City of London. The arched building at water level is the former Billingsgate Market, which became the "home of fresh fish and foul language" in 1877. The market has since been relocated to a more suitable position in Docklands.

Right A view from the high walkway of Tower Bridge showing the high rise buildings of London's financial district, with the Tower at the bottom right and St Paul's Cathedral at the extreme left.

Left While many bridges have disappeared without trace from the river - including one that has been re-assembled in Arizona - the red piers of the former London, Chatham and Dover railway company river-crossing are still standing, stranded between Blackfriars road and rail bridges. It was thought that their removal would create extra turbulence for river traffic.

Left The London, Chatham and Dover railway company's coat of arms and insignia has, however, been preserved, surmounting one of the red piers.

Above Modern architecture near the river at Docklands, on a piece of land known as the Isle of Dogs. This once-marshy area is thought to have got its name from the hounds that Henry VIII used when hunting here. Now developers have given it a new life as an extension of the City of London, downriver from Tower Bridge.

Left The busy river passing the City is framed by the ornate balustrade of Tower Bridge.

Above and below left Further downstream, although still facing the Isle of Dogs, is Wren's Royal Naval College. The Queen's House (distant, in the centre of both pictures) was designed by Inigo Jones in 1637 and is one of the oldest buildings still standing in London. While the Docklands development has transformed the opposite bank, the river frontage at Greenwich is still as Wren conceived it.

Above and above right In the former cargo hold of the *Cutty Sark* is a museum
containing a fine collection of figureheads from the bows of 19th century
sailing ships. Many sailors believed that it was unlucky to sail without one. The figures
are sometimes portraits of heroes, and sometimes of the shipowner or his wife.
The figure of Omar Pasha (this page, right) is from a brig built in 1854
and is unusual in having glass eyes.

Left The *Cutty Sark* in dry dock at Greenwich was the fastest ship in the world when she was launched in 1869, with a top speed of 17 knots. Originally intended for the tea trade routes to China, she was later shifted to the Australian wool trade, but the opening of the Suez Canal and the improved technology of steam-driven ships meant that her days were numbered.

Tower Bridge, seen
here at dusk when
there is still some
activity on the river.

INDEX

OPENING TIMES

Henry VII's magnificent late Gothic 'English Perpendicular' style chapel, at the east end of Westminster Abbey, is one of London's outstanding sights that can be visited at the times shown below. The statue on the right is of George V.

Royal Botanic Gardens, Kew
Garden: daily 9.30am - sunset
Greenhouses: daily 10.00am - sunset

Brick Lane Market
Sun 6.00am - 1.00pm

British Library, St. Pancras
Reading rooms and interior: apply to Visitors' Centre, tel. 0171 412 7332
Courtyard and piazza: open during daylight hours

Brixton Arcade Market
Mon - Tues and Thurs - Sat 8.00am - 5.30pm, Wed 8.00am - 1.00pm

Buckingham Palace
Aug - early Oct, daily 9.30am - 4.00pm, but dates vary and should be confirmed on tel.0171 839 1377.

Camden Lock Market
Sat - Sun 10.00am - 6.00pm

Chelsea Physic Garden, Royal Hospital Road
5 Apr - 25 Oct, Wed 12.00pm - 5.00pm, Sun 2.00pm - 6.00pm; also special Snowdrop openings (Feb) and in Chelsea Flower Show Week (May), tel. 0171 352 5646

Chiswick House, Burlington Lane
House: Apr - Sept, daily 10.00am - 6.00pm; Oct - Mar, Wed - Sun 10.00am - 4.00pm
Grounds: open during daylight hours

Columbia Road Flower Market
Sun 8.00am - 2.00pm

Cutty Sark, Greenwich
Apr - Sept, Mon - Sat 10.00am - 6.00pm, Sun 12.00am - 6.00pm
Oct - Mar, Mon - Sat 10.00am - 5.00pm, Sun 12.00am - 5.00pm

Hampton Court Palace
State Apartments: mid Mar - mid Oct, Tues - Sun 9.30am - 6.00pm, Mon 10.15am - 6.00pm; mid Oct - mid Mar, Tues - Sun 9.30am - 4.30pm, Mon 10.15am - 4.30pm
Grounds: open during daylight hours

Highgate Cemetery, Swains Lane
For opening times tel. 0181 340 1834
Admission to West side is by guided tour only

Horniman Museum and Gardens, London Road, Forest Hill
Museum: Mon - Sat 10.30am - 5.30pm, Sun 2.00pm - 5.30pm
Gardens: open during daylight hours

Middle Temple Hall and Gardens
For opening times tel. 0171 353 4355

Royal Naval College, Greenwich
Daily 2.30pm - 4.45pm

Houses of Parliament
Tours can be arranged through your Member of Parliament. The Visitors' Galleries are open when the Houses are sitting: for dates and times tel. 0171 219 4272 (Commons) or 0171 219 3107 (Lords). Both Houses are closed in Easter Week, July - Oct, and for 3 weeks at Christmas

Pet Cemetery, Hyde Park, at Victoria Gate
Open by special appointment only: tel. 0171 298 2100

Petticoat Lane Market, Middlesex St, E1
Sun 9.00am - 2.00pm

Porchester Spa, Queensway
Separate opening times for men, women, and mixed couples: tel. 0171 792 3980

Portobello Market, Portobello Road
Sat 8.00am - 5.30pm

Queen's House, Greenwich
Daily 10.00am - 5.00pm

St. Paul's Cathedral
Mon - Sat 8.30am - 4.00pm

Sir John Soane's Museum, Lincoln's Inn Fields.
Tues - Sat 10.00am - 5.00pm

Spencer House, St. James's Place
Guided tours only, Sun 10.30am - 4.45pm, Closed Jan and Aug

Stratford Town Hall
Old Time Dancing on Monday afternoon. For dates and times tel. 0181 534 7835

Strawberry Hill, Waldegrave Road, Twickenham
Guided tours only, Apr - Oct, Sun 2.00pm - 4.30pm. May be open at other times by special arrangement: tel. 0181 240 4000

Syon House, Brentford
Apr - Oct, Wed - Sun 11.00am - 5.00pm

Tate Gallery, Millbank
Daily 10.00am - 5.30pm
Closed 24 - 26 Dec

Temple Church, Temple Lane
Daily 10.00am - 4.00pm

Tower Bridge (incl. high walkway)
Apr - Oct, daily 10.00am - 6.30pm; Nov - Mar, daily 9.30am - 5.15pm

Tower of London
Mar - Oct, Mon - Sat 9.00am - 5.00pm, Sun 10 - 5.00pm
Nov - Feb, Tues - Sat 9.00am - 4.00pm, Sun - Mon 10.00am - 4.00pm

Wat Buddhapadipa Temple, Calonne Road, Wimbledon.
Sat - Sun 9.00am - 6.00pm

Westminster Abbey
Mon - Fri 9.15am - 3.45pm, Sat 9.00am - 2.00pm, 3.45pm - 5.00pm

York House Gardens, Twickenham.
Open during daylight hours

PHOTOGRAPHER'S ACKNOWLEDGMENTS

Special thanks are due to Maria Grasso and Jim Pedersen, for their invaluable design and editorial contribution.

Many others have helped in numerous ways, both directly and indirectly. I am particularly grateful to the following, who are listed in alphabetical order :

Mike Allen, Rupert Asquith, Andrea Belloli, Nigel Best, Simon and Julia Blunt, Vaughan Clarke, Paula Conneely, Martin Day, Andrew Delaney, Roger Emery, Noreen Evans, Belinda and Tim Farnfield, Dan Fleming, Alison Follis, George Goodson, Colin Grant, Claire Hobday, Alhaj Zillul Hoque, Charles Ironside, Annette Kyriakides, Mark Laughton, Phrakru Lom, Debrett Lyons, Jenny Mitchell, Louise Muddle, Jean Pateman, Carolyn Payter, Chris Oliver, Kate Pocock, The Rev. Donald Reeves, Mrs. L.Rentall, King Richard, Jane Rick, Ted Robbins, the Roney family, Helen St. Cyr, Claire Sawford, Lorna Sizer, Richard Smith, Paula Stevens, Marja Vuorio, Peter Willasey, Luisa Zinn.